Greed: A Confession

GREED:

a confession

POEMS BY
D.R. Goodman

ABLE MUSE PRESS

Able Muse Press

www.ablemusepress.com

Printed in the United States of America

Library of Congress Control Number: 2014914717

ISBN 978-1-927409-38-1 (paperback)
ISBN 978-1-927409-37-4 (digital)

Cover design by Alexander Pepple,
            adapted from the image "frog stock 199" by hatestock

Book design by Alexander Pepple

Able Muse Press is an imprint of *Able Muse:* A Review of Poetry, Prose & Art—at www.ablemuse.com

Able Muse Press
467 Saratoga Avenue #602
San Jose, CA 95129

for Marian,

in memory

Acknowledgments

I am grateful to the editors of the following journals where many of these poems originally appeared, sometimes in earlier versions.

Able Muse: "The Face of Things" (winner, 2013 Able Muse Write Prize for Poetry), "No Love Lost," "Out Late in Summer," "A Red-Tailed Hawk Patrols."

Apalachee Review: "Supernumerary Limbs."

Birmingham Poetry Review: "False Cattleguard."

Buckle&: "Fugu."

Carquinez Poetry Review: "A Homeopathy of the Spirit."

Cold Mountain Review: "Greed: A Confession."

Confluence: "Lest I Forget You."

Controlled Burn: "One's Own Kind."

Crazyhorse: "Owls in the City Hills."

Crucible: "Simplicity Itself."

Cumberland Poetry Review: "Dark Matter," "Searching for the Slave Graveyard," "Serena."

Distillery: "Signs and Symbols."

Eclipse: "A Certain Joy."

The Formalist: "Crystalline," "Desires Are Interchangeable," "The Question of Suicides at Niagara Falls."

Hampden-Sydney Poetry Review: "Seasonal Song."

Hawaii Pacific Review: "Pigeon, Rock Dove."

Iambs and Trochees: "The Goats Laboring."

Illuminations: "Barn Swallows at Point Reyes."

Limestone: "Interstate 80 Eclipse."

Lullwater Review: "Scargate."

Measure: "Waking on the Northwest Slope."

Meridian Anthology of Contemporary Poetry: "Burr."

Notre Dame Review: "Odilon Redon at the Musée d'Orsay."

Pebble Lake Review: "Autumn in a Place without Winter."

The Quotable: "Birds by the Bay."

Red Wheelbarrow: "A Blackened Pot, a Bone, a Pair of Pliers."

Seattle Review: "Love Sonnet."

South Carolina Review: "Gradients."

South Dakota Review: "Vision of a White Bird."

Tampa Review: "December Meditation. "

Water-Stone Review: "Science Fair."

West Wind Review: "Abstracts: On Some Paintings in a Room," "Starlight, Mountains," "Wakened by a Cricket at Dark, Jerusalem, 1975."

Whitefish Review: "Hawk."

Wisconsin Review: "The Solipsist at Rush Hour."

Worcester Review: "Burnscape."

Foreword

Depth cannot hide. And so it flutters, sings,
betrays itself upon the face of things.

D.R. Goodman may be greedy, as she confesses and demonstrates in her richly rewarding poems, but she donates all the proceeds. Like a prospector hitting pay dirt, she revels in the "spill of gold, as in a pirate's dream/ cascading down my driveway." But like the canny, subtle artist that she proves herself to be, she capitalizes on her discoveries and immediately starts making connections, linking images, contrasting the windfall of yellow gingko leaves with the wedding ring she wears. Those images appear in the book's last poem, "Clair de Lune," which encapsulates many of her themes: evanescence, the bounty of nature, the presence of love or love lost, and the eagerness to pursue the "heroic, dangerous quests of greed and sin."

The title poem, "Greed: A Confession," serves as prologue to the book's four sections, but it's really more of an overture to an internal drama's four acts. It consists of three sonnets (the first of over two dozen in the book), each arranged as two quatrains and two tercets, each beginning with "Once," each confessing a particular instance of greed, all three linked together as one poem without numbers or any interruptions except for stanza breaks, something like what James Merrill does with a string of sonnets in "Days of 1971." Each sonnet names some object of desire that multiplies as the speaker seizes it: a toad, a handful of strawberries, a coin found in a laundromat. She acknowledges that "the seed/ of avarice possessed me" but discovers "the more we tasted, the more came into view." It is an ironic confession by a seeker who gladly stakes a claim to "this new-// discovered seam of riches, which we mined/ by inch and yard." She exults in the "glee/ of larceny" with a "deep and greedy smile."

What she actually declares is her generosity, the flip side of avarice, which we learn about on the fifth ledge in Dante's *Purgatorio,* where the sinners lie face down on the ground, as their eyes had been fixed on earthly things. Along with gluttony and lust, it's one of the deadly sins caused by loving something too much. D.R. Goodman is greedy for things of this world—not in the rapacious, bottom-line manner of plutocrats, misers, and Wall Street brokers but for the enlightenment of the senses and the enrichment of her poetry. She's sharing the wealth she accumulates.

As the book proceeds, two things are immediately apparent and especially striking: Goodman's mastery of traditional poetic form and the way she intersperses poems in free verse among the metrical work. The intensification of language in her rhymed iambic poems gives way gracefully to the loosening in her unmeasured lines. The casual back-and-forth between the fixity and flux of the two modes produces a wave-like rhythm within her oceanic book. The voice remains the same, but the register changes, as it does in James Wright's final collection, *This Journey,* which includes poems in free verse, meter, and prose. In *Greed,* it feels liturgical, the way hymns and anthems alternate with Biblical readings, prayers, and a sermon within a church service. It's an orchestral effect, as in J.S. Bach's cantatas.

Animals outnumber people in these poems: hummingbird, pigeon, egret, vulture, barn swallow, bat, raccoon, cow, puffer fish, two kinds of frog, donkey, goose, robin, luna moth, cicada, dragonfly, cardinal, a "Red Sea sponge." But there are recurring characters, such as the red-tailed hawk on patrol, making "Easy circles, yes, but never *lazy*—/ those lyrics have it wrong—each careless arc/ an engine at its heart, a rust-red flame/ of blood-red purpose." Goodman never sentimentalizes her creatures. Scientific exactitude is part of her method, and she's strict about the veracity of her symbols, the annihilating power of the great bird whose flight we admire:

> How sweet the images we call on,
> of parachutes and gliders: human stock;
> we dream ourselves beneath her wings and fly,
> forgetting beak, forgetting spur and talon.

Goodman's knack for metaphor is one of her trademarks, as when she describes a flock of vultures "wheeling and climbing/ like kids/ in the hills/ on bikes" or notices how owls "hunt us,/ casting their deep vowels like feathered hooks" or reveals how a wood frog "dons gelid winter/ like a topcoat/ of porcelain glaze."

Her most remarkable poem about animals is "The Goats Laboring," two long stanzas in rhymed couplets about how goats are "Trucked in like migrant workers, spindly legged/ and eager, they assault the hill—once logged,/ now thick with stumps and brush, and tinder-dry/ brown grass...." The greed of their hunger will serve to fight brush fires. Goodman notes the traditional association of goats, "this cloven-hoofed and horned and bearded horde," with the Satanic. But like the hawk (and Blake's tiger), they are really paragons of energy, which the poet-painter called "eternal delight," finishing their job and transforming the hill in a single day, "the grass completely cropped;/ the laborers about in varied poses,/ most lying, ruminating; some with noses/ thrust deep in troughs of water or of feed/ that supplements their diet of dry weeds." The images are hilarious and delightful, some goats posing on stumps, some "rampant" and stretching "to reach forbidden tips/ of juniper and oak," some locking horns "like classic wrestlers on an ancient urn." The poem ends with a quintessential old goat that's faced with mortal danger at the limits of experience, a note that's struck repeatedly throughout the book:

> One elder turns on us a slit-eyed stare
> of startling blue, his curly sheep-like hair,
> an old man's coat. He seeks new leaves, so dense
> and green just past the wires, but stops to sense
> the tick, tick, tick of the electric fence.

In Goodman's free-verse sestina, "Signs and Symbols," the narrative is so clear, vivid, and compelling that the form becomes transparent, like an invisible fence that keeps a dog in the yard—and lets passersby get a more immediate view of the animal presence. It's about a couple returning home from a funeral to discover that "the tall eucalyptus has toppled down/ our steep back slope, its great crown of leaves/ filling what should have been the bright/ sky above our patio, branches bowed taut against the glass/ of the kitchen window and sliding door." A marvelous epiphany comes to the speaker when the "you," her beloved, shares a realization:

> how the highest limbs scraped down
> the side of the house, leaving a bright
> green trail that passes right over the doorbell
> button. *It rang the bell!*—you laugh and tap on the glass
> for me, and I leave
> the green quiet of the kitchen to come see
>
> the evidence—the sound of a downed tree falling: no crash, nor breaking glass,
> but the bright sound of a doorbell in an empty house, leaving
> the faintest echo, its mark on the door, a shimmer in the air that only you can see.

The end of the sestina shows off Goodman's sly sense of humor as it answers the question of whether a tree makes a sound when it falls unnoticed in a forest.

In addition to her formal expertise, Goodman is a sharp-eyed, curious observer who meditates deeply on what she notices. As Marianne Moore, another astute observer of animals, says in "The Pangolin," "To explain grace requires/ a curious hand." In "Vision of a White Bird," Goodman articulates the grace in how "heavy branch and tree/ float light as cumulus, and slender bird/ grows steady and immovable, unstirred/ by fifteen knots of breeze." In "Seasonal Song," she asks, in language similar to Moore's, "What warm and spiny hope, what tiny glow/ now kindles like a phosphorescent cell,/ pale bioluminescence on a swell/ of steely inner sea?"

Places matter profoundly too, as in her frequent evocations of the California coast and her trio of poems about Jerusalem, the "City of Dust" where "Even on *shabbat,* jets thundered overhead." In "Searching for the Slave Graveyard," Goodman returns to Oak Ridge, Tennessee, but discovers "how quickly it dissolved/ and left us turning, questioning and lost." The past may not be retrievable, but the present is, so she exults in how "We circled on,/ and marked a boulder streaked with quartz, and paused// to taste a wild persimmon's fallen fruit." Even in the vicinity of the lost graveyard of slaves and the "viewing ground that overlooked the dark/ refinery that helped construct the bomb," a moment of Edenic pleasure can emerge.

D.R. Goodman is adept at celebration, recognizing that "There is a certain joy/ that depends on nothing." And just as Shakespeare urges us "To love that well which thou must leave ere long" and Wallace Stevens declares that "Death is the mother of beauty," she also recognizes that human joy depends on an urgency that's rooted in the nothingness of death, the Grim Reaper whom she glimpses on the street and in whose scythe she still sees the glimmering of beauty:

> If you met a stranger, his face obscured
> in the hood of his night-black cowl,
> you would say, "How the sun glints
> on the beautiful curve of your blade."

—John Drury

Contents

II

III

IV

Greed: A Confession

Greed: A Confession

Once as a child, I came upon a toad
so tiny it could rest upon my nail,
so fresh from metamorphosis—not frail,
but delicate, exposed—and as it rode

my finger for a moment I was flush
with power and delight; and when it leapt
to reach the mossy ground, I'd intercept
and capture it again, till in the hush

and shadow of the evening woods there came
another, and another, hopping down
across the trail—a hundred of the same

exquisite, tiny creatures; and the seed
of avarice possessed me, drew me down
to hands and knees in happiness and greed.

Once as a youth, I stumbled in a field
where berries ripened, hidden in the shade
of soft, serrated leaves; and as we played
our sultry summer games, they came revealed

as tiny flecks of red along the ground,
that bruised between our fingers, left a sweet,
dark stain, and such an aura in the heat
of wild strawberry wine—until we found

the more we tasted, more came into view
beneath the low-grown foliage; and soon
we stripped our shirts to gather in this new-

discovered seam of riches, which we mined
by inch and yard, not pausing till the moon
turned light to gray and left us color blind.

Once in a basement laundromat, I gleaned
a fallen coin from off the linty floor,
and rising, caught the glint of seven more
below the broken slot of a machine;

and though they were not mine, and weren't much,
I bent to find a way to work them free
with fingernails and wire, feeling a glee
of larceny shoot through me at the touch

of silver in my hand. And on the streets
again, with pocket full of change, I smiled
a deep and greedy smile—not for the sweets

a coin could buy, but for my liberty
in such a fatted world, and for the child
grown full in it by guileless thievery.

I

A Certain Joy

There is a certain joy
that depends on nothing.
One inhabits it.

It is there in the day
when you walk out,
whether chill and gray
or magnified by light,
and you inhale it.

Now it is in your blood,
and it fills you to the skin,
wraps a tightness around your heart.

It is in you, yes,
and equally in the world,
where it speaks from the darkest rose
in your neighbor's garden,
or the bright metallic flash
of an absurdly tiny bird,
copper and green and red
in the glinting air.

The city streets are miraculous,
how they wind downhill through the trees;
the smell of smoke from the houses
sweet nostalgia.
This in spite of everything.

If you met a stranger, his face obscured
in the hood of his night-black cowl,
you would say, "How the sun glints
on the beautiful curve of your blade."

The Face of Things

The eye knows leaf from hummingbird at once,
even at distance, even dusk; discerns
among the flecks of green an immanence
of sudden flight, as though the will returns

a subtle wavelength, visible as light.
The green of foliage, the leafy green
of matching feather, then a clever sleight
of surface that conveys a deeper scene,

the heartbeat underneath. The eye both *in*
and *measuring* the world—an inborn task
that even camouflage won't contravene
cannot help pointing back behind the mask.

Depth cannot hide. And so it flutters, sings,
betrays itself upon the face of things.

Science Fair

This
is a vertebra
from a cow.

Big as my hands,
this bare bone,
bleached and parched
by its time
in the desert sun—

notice
the transverse process,
the spinous process,
the vertebral foramen,

that tube through which
the spinal cord would run,
like a necklace wire,
or a string of lights,
sparking and humming
with life.

Here
it is a lost bead,
its beauty
not accidental:
these sculpted curves

and polished holes
for the passage of nerves
and blood—

in a scatter of weathered stones,
it would announce itself,
familiar.

So it did, when we came
hunting arrowheads:
a white spill of bones
dispersed on a hummock of sand.

I was small enough.
I crouched
in the arching ribcage,
held a leg bone
in my two hands.
The skull too heavy
to drag by its horn
back home,
I took, instead,
this vertebra:

once a part
of a swaying spine
that was hung
with a hammock of cow,
who ambled among

arrowheads, and ate;
and saw, perhaps,
the stars at night, white
and scattered like bones;
and died at last
a simple
or an awful death.

Now, here,
plain and labeled,
no blinking lights,
nor fancy models:

this
is a vertebra
from a cow.

It speaks for itself.
It will win no prize.
It is just the childish wonder
from which the rest derives.

Pigeon, Rock Dove

There is evidence some birds can see the stars in daylight.
           – Nick Brent, Eyesign and the Homing Instinct

What other secrets have you, claret-eyed,
pin-headed genius in disguise? I can't
but see you with new eyes. So oddly slant
of step, so slovenly of nest, you hide
your pied blue brilliance cleverly astride
this daftly cooing clumsiness, beak bent
to pecking pavement, soiling as you hunt
discarded seeds and scraps. And yet, inside
that feathered skull the universe is drawn
in fine magnetic clouds, in starry sky
and subtle shifts of light, in infrared;
and eyeing me, it seems, even at noon,
you see the breadth of space, and wonder why
I cling so tightly to my crust of bread.

Vision of a White Bird

An egret quits a cypress branch in wind,
turns in a swirling gust, and lights again,
asserts its brilliant white against the green
of layered, cloud-like limbs—and so begins
a strange inversion: heavy branch and tree
float light as cumulus, and slender bird
grows steady and immovable, unstirred
by fifteen knots of breeze. What gravity
can hold a thing so ready for the air,
all stilt and neck and feather, too refined
for solid ground? How can the wind not fill
and lift it like a silken kite?—the pair
so similar and slight, but for a mind,
a laser-focused eye, the weight of will.

The Question of Suicides at Niagara Falls

Not why they go, but how we stay on shore,
one instant from the current's breathless pull,
its power palpable, hypnotic, full
of nature's swift relentlessness. And more:
how anyone can live for miles from here—
this undercurrent draining, like a dull,
hard weight on every spirit, and the chill
of ominous, gray rapids always near,
forever sweeping downward, toward the roar
and plume of some calamity. The force
of dizzying descent, the edge, compels:
one's mind, like any raft, swept to the core,
must ride this glassy water on its course
of rapid no return. We grip the rails.

Night Comes, with Fireflies

Dusk doesn't fall, but rises, like a fine,
dark net that's lain in folds beneath the day—
the foot of every wood—and when the slant
of sun grows weak, is hoisted by the night
to mask its coming. Tiny flicks of light
ride softly, slowly, up before a bank
of fading trees and vines, a scattered play
of pinpoint flashes, fleeting by design,
to draw our shallow focus to the pale
periphery, distract us in a chase
for evanescent gold, while there behind
the blinking screen, a darkness of a kind
we'd near forgotten, black as starless space,
consumes the land, the trees, its own black veil.

Owls in the City Hills

                          —how they hunt us,
casting their deep vowels like feathered hooks,
to pull us from shallow sleep or simple talk,
and out to the night, the stand of eucalyptus

a looming silhouette, the black above us;
we, barefoot on the littered deck, and blind,
stare wide into the dark and hear the sound
move eerily from tree to tree around us;

our backs to the spreading net of city lights
below, we've nothing but the trees, our eyes,
the dark, the sound, these owls we cannot see—

though once at dusk, by chance, I saw one light
and spread its wings, and, tinged by copper skies,
lay silence to the city, utterly.

Exiting the Night

By living late, and sleeping late, we miss
the moment when the bats come home to roost—
when crooked shadows flit in jagged loops
that seem to seek the chimney, seem to miss,

then somehow disappear into the eaves;
and they (the bats) tuck wing to fur to wing
in crevices and roof-beam beveling,
doze through our nearly diametric lives,

invisible as brown on brown—until
today, wakened by dreams, I caught a slight,
compelling corner-glimpse in gray first light,

of sudden motion in the mostly still
new dawn; and drawn, I rose to see the flight:
our dark companions exiting the night.

Barn Swallows at Point Reyes

We who hunch here
huddled in the cold
envy the swallows, perched
one to next
in the upper gap of the shelter,
under the two-inch eaves.

Dawn finds them parked there,
a row of beaks
like odd little smiles,
sleek deep blue
and orange-brown,
rich colors of a glossy print.

The wind that whips the camp
is their accustomed air.
As we pull close our coats,
clutch at our loose
and knotted, sand-blown hair,
suddenly

they drop, free-fall, and bullet out
across the misty field,
wings from nowhere
and those jet-streak tails,
skimming the gale
like reckless skiffs on the sea.

Hummingbirds

They're cute; they're small;
you get on with your life!
　　　　　—M. May

Clearly, she does not understand
the hours of bright, repetitive pleasure,
the long days spent with my work
at the kitchen table, distracted,
fidgeting, piqued with delight,
turning my head at the thrum,
the deep hum through the open screen
of this emerald green, this rapid airborne leaf
zeroing in for a perch.
　　　　　　　　I no longer call
for her to come, see, it has alit,
the blur of wings slowed to a twitch
then folded, perfect, on sleek-suited sides,
head thrown back and tilting side to side
with its little tune, really no more
than a drawn-out squeak, flashing its metal
ruby throat to the sun.
　　　　　　　　Even the cat
has grown bored, yawned and wound his stripes
into tight-packaged sleep, and I'm alone
to look up again with that same thrill—
again—for my brain has gone slick,
and I cannot arrive at ennui.

She'd agree, I think,
that my thick, unstinting glee is akin
to what that patient has, the contented one
on the neurology ward, who cannot remember,
cannot at all get on with her life,
and happily reads, again and again,
chapter one of her favorite book.

Vulture Flock

Not enough death today
for the vultures
so they clown together
wheeling and climbing
like kids
in the hills
on bikes

spread-fingered
V-winged they
teeter and glide
buzzard-circles
spiral wide and
down and
down to a
point

then skim among
the houses
so close
their size amazes
casting shadows
big as planes
a child
cranes to see
as small dogs scatter
they clatter and land
gather on a roof
in a group

O black cabal
O boders of ill
flesh-red faces terrible
in daylight
wings spread and raised
like capes
a row of sun-drenched draculas

startling the neighbors
till shade comes
and one by one
they fold
move edgeward
lean their weight
on a draft
and swoop away
like shadows

switching back
through the trees
toward a distant roar
the freeway sound
which to us
means travel
to them
means skunk
or possum,
even deer.

The Solipsist at Rush Hour

Alone in traffic; dusk; each metal shell
like Chuang Tzu's empty boat; nerves to the wheel,
I navigate between blameless machines
that merge and pass along a concrete stream,

perspective lodged within this driven vessel
at center of the freeway's mythic riddle:
a thousand wheels with only a single *I*.

What proof of other drivers? Would it lie
in shared direction, signals we engage
with meaning, gestures recognized as rage?

Or wordplay: There can be no *accidents*
        without *purposes*.
No, the lone headlight beams from here,
        and it meets only surfaces.

Lift the other crumpled hood: you'll find
just wire and metal, movement, smoke and sound;
a pump, maybe—pulsing like a heart.
The headlamp is a bulb: take it apart,

there's no getting inside it—not the way
I'm in my head beam, inescapably,
alone in evening traffic with my own seeing eyes,

this view so singular, so sole and only,
it almost makes the throat clutch,
almost makes the carburetor catch.

Breakdown

It's when memory collapses
that human machinery
is most bared.
Things don't mesh:
ideas pronounced with certainty
meet awkward stares;
the flesh cannot accept
the simplest commands—
a belt becomes a puzzle,
a razor loses meaning in one's hands.
There is an almost audible
grinding of gears,
of thought scraping down
through a knot of aluminized wires.
We expect such breakdowns
in cars, but not in ours—that is,
in those whom we have loved,
in whose eyes we thought the sparks
meant spirit.
With the car, we did not
hurry it aside, abashed,
buckled by the loss,
fearing for our own internal works.

Interstate 80 Eclipse

Moonrise traffic; taillights slow and jam
the shoreline, as a brilliant disc appears,
slides up behind the hills, and finally clears
the easterly horizon. By the time
I round the curve, merge north along the bay,
a perfect slip of shadow mars its side,
a finger-arc of blackness poised to slide
its silver coin across the blue-black sky.
The shadow grows in increments, the dark
precision of it ominous and clear
at once: for just a moment, I'm aware
of planets in their motion, and a spark
of sunlight as it passes through the night
to strike the moon from hiding. Here I drive
past cypress trees where snowy egrets perch
like candles; and a heron on a rail
leans down toward the eerie crescent light
reflected on an inlet, pitched to dive
should any moonstruck fish rise up to touch
the lunar surface in its shifting veil.

Starlight, Mountains

Some evenings, looking out across the pass,
one can mistake a porch light for a star;
a common lamp of filament and glass
will shine with such a clarity that Mars
and Venus seem its match; and it will rise
as if to trail its billion brethren there
into the crowded, turning, star-spilt skies
one only sees at altitude—thin air
and isolation sharpening the night.

Already the horizon is erased,
rock cliffs and snowfields liquefied to black,
stark mountain summits easily effaced
by nightfall; and within this liquid dark,
the pressure underneath one's feet the last
surviving frame of reference, in a world
of space, and pinpoint lights, glittering past
infinity—the Milky Way unfurled
from here, by one bright star and simple sight.

A pity to discover the mistake—
that star too fixed, too steady, holding low
upon the pass, when, higher, toward the peaks,
a subtle movement and the faintest glow—
enough to bring the mountain rushing back
in all its cold solidity: a jeep
negotiating switchbacks in the dark,

tight to the cliffs, inching along a steep
descent, a trail more suited for a mule,
the tension visible miles from the tracks;
just one missed tread, and that small, shining jewel
would be a falling star, throwing off sparks
of accidental beauty, until light.

II

Odilon Redon at the Musée d'Orsay

Pastels, early 1900s

Part of the mystery
is in the room itself,
darkened and set apart;
the works set apart again
behind glass; the atmosphere
regulated; a universe
delineated—captured space
with separate natural laws.

So it is that Apollo's white horses,
broad and muscular,
can rise like clouds across the sky;
so it is
that a frail old man
stands earthbound,
burdened with wings.

In this world, matter
is created and destroyed
by the gesture of a hand,
stasis made vivid,
luminous;
ashes to charcoal, dust to light,
a light so real
it escapes its wooden frame
and infuses the room like a mist—

like the filtered light
of this brilliant stained-glass window,
deep blue and gold
and casting its glow
in a somber charcoal church—
the bright glass lit
by artifice, from behind,
by a hidden sun.

In another frame,
it makes bright a distant landscape:
a candescent world
of blue and earthy green,
shimmering with gold,
and Buddha stands serene,
hand open, inward looking,
signaling what is everywhere—

this golden light,
in bits of gold leaf
peeling like bark from a tree,
caught on the wind, in the air;
they spread to the gold-leaf frame
and into the darkened room,
swirl through the light and shadows,
settle in the patrons' hair.

Abstracts: On Some Paintings in a Room

"The Sound of Ku" by Sono Osato

1. Synecdoche

Having distilled the yellow of the bright desert
and laid it thick and textured
on a swatch of stretched cloth,
somehow she gave us landscape.
And on approach it prisms
into every shade of sand and shadow,
stone and hollow, camouflage and light,
the dust-streaked floor of any wash or wadi,
swept by rain and brushed with minerals and life.
This one square inch a thousand times enlarged;
this swath of canyon, pebble-strewn and washed;
this whole, great, yellow, heat-lit, bright expanse,
viewed from a stellar distance: here at once
is all of these, at any height and layer,
and each the same, and every part the whole.

2. Incantation on the Dark Works

How we treasure our cuts and losses.
How every black mark becomes ashes.
How any red fleck, a hot ember.
How smoke permeates and still lingers.
How what was burdens more than what's present.

How what's rust carves its way to what isn't.
How we press on a nerve till it passes.
How we treasure our cuts and our losses.

3. Sonnet: White on Gray

Snow on boughs; a blizzard—these are what
we must perceive, what every simple mind
must see in any layering of white
on gray; and now the work is all behind
the painted surface: deep into the walls,
a scene that grows for miles, invisible
with evergreens enswirled in winter falls
of spinning, weighted white—and audible
in that strange way of snow-thick atmosphere,
as if it seals the world, creates a shift
in pressure and a humming in the ear,
or absence of a humming, or as if
some chemistry precipitates all sound,
and sends it falling silent to the ground.

4. Close-ups in Brown

Mud is the sound of spring, the sound of fall,
the sodden ground of life. This wax and oil,
this luscious piling on of umber muck,
enshrines a molten mass of muddy track
in rain-soaked woods: imagine a surround
of fallen leaves like hands pressed to the ground,

decaying autumn colors soaked to brown,
in clay-dark rivulets that trickle down
and ripple, catching earth and bits of moss
and fern, the green dissolving. Here—come close;
a hint of something lost: a copper fleck,
an iridescent beetle's wing, a slick
of oily film, metallic rainbow dulled
by dirt. Look closer still: the underside
must almost seethe with movement, almost roil
with coprophilic creatures of the soil,
at work on nature's waste, and on this wall.

Burnscape

Destruction
lets us see things
through a new ocular—
like dissection,
only more spectacular.
Not the wonder
of the inner workings, whole;
but the oddity
of one chipped bone, alone,
blackened among ashes—
as after an explosion,
in a puzzling tangle
of what.
Here a tool, molten,
fused to its neighbor,
a strange hybrid
of jaws. Or the heart
of some appliance, the part
you would never see,
bared.
The reasoning backward
is a revelation—
how these changed fragments
retain the power
to project their former shapes:
wrench, pliers,

blender, house; the shrub
whose roots once filled
these snaking holes;
the raccoon
crouching under it.

A Blackened Pot, a Bone, a Pair of Pliers

Of all the shards we salvaged from the fire,
one shone among the ashes in my palm:
a crystal lens that held the world entire

within its lucid eye. I held it higher,
and viewed the wreckage in its sooty realm,
and all the shards we salvaged from the fire:

odd lumps of metal, burnt piano wire
(the wood and ivory vanished in the kiln),
this crystal lens that held the world entire—

a phoenix eye that glittered in the pyre
to witness all it once had played on film
reduced to shards we salvaged from the fire:

a blackened pot, a bone, a pair of pliers,
the barrel of a gun; and in my palm,
this crystal lens. I held the world entire

refracted there; I held it to the fiery
sun above the city, bright and calm,
relighting what we salvaged from the fire:
a crystal lens that held the world entire.

Hawk

Where stands of eucalyptus burned to sticks,
and stood a year like spears into the air
with blackened shafts—and then another year—
till some deep urge to life burst in their trunks

and broke them into leaf—not limb by limb,
but all along the burn-scarred lengths of bark
a coat of leaves, with barren branches, stark
as bleaching bones, left bare; where, ten years in,

the tallest tree still wears a jagged spire
of naked, sun-worn wood above its crown:
there sits the regal, rugged hawk—so high

he must command great cities, and the bay,
the sea—and casts his razor eye just down
to one unlucky pigeon on a wire.

False Cattleguard

The cows disappoint.
That will to greener pastures—
stopped short by a painted-on grate,
bovine *trompe l'oeil.*
And we had so admired
the slow current of their wisdom—
accepting as impassable
the genuine gaps and rails,
on the weight of self-knowledge:
wobbly hooves, delicate hocks.
Now they are made fools,
gathered in loose groups,
moon-eyed and thwarted,
at the slant end of the fence—
much as we might gather
at the wide-spaced slats of change,
unable to risk a step.

Burr

How did the pod know
a small spiked spiral,
suitable to catch on cloth,
was the way to success?
That any creature,
furred or clothed,
would pass?
That this young girl,
harried by the sticker
between sock and moccasin
would stop, unhurried,
to work it free,
admire its spiny elegance,
and in a spark
of shared intelligence,
plant it on a far oasis of grass?

Fugu

*The human species holds more than 75%
of its genes in common with the puffer fish.*

Sometimes, there's an inkling:
a tickling behind the jaw,
a tingling in awkward limbs,
an involuntary blotchiness
of skin in the patchy light
that scatters down through treetops
as through ocean;
a certain notion of simple
round-faced shock,
spikes on end
to ward off those who prey;
sometimes,
a touch of poison
to make them pay.

Supernumerary Limbs

*When a salamander's regenerating limb bud is cut,
rotated, and grafted back onto the stump, a normal limb
will develop, sometimes with smaller supernumerary
limbs appearing at predictable locations along the graft.*

The stump buds like a dogwood,
dense with its pattern of stem or leaf or limb—

with a kind of knowledge: when cut,
to flower into flesh and bone,

a fine spotted leg, a fan of tiny fingers,
slow, unfolding, intricate and simple as a scar.

We, gods of manipulation, coveting this power,
spin the bud like a dial, crack the vault—

left, then right, each number or notch a cell;
willing through our chance combinations

that nature should spill her secrets—and she does:
in salamander digits, slick and damp,

on bony limbs akimbo and askew,
waving a comic gesture, one that sends

us all the mocking promise that we too
may one day sprout such tiny, useless hands.

Scargate

Is it healing—
or something more sinister—
when a cut closes up
without a trace?
No truth-exposing cicatrix;
key witnesses
conveniently erased—
by means too shadowy
to interrupt. It's something
in the nature of a cover-up.

Dark Matter

The past is forever with me, and I remember it all.
    —*Nien Ching,* Life and Death in Shanghai

One wonders how she rises—how *we* rise—
under the weight of it. Or bear the cost
of wholeness, as its burden multiplies
on end—to let no memory be lost,
no loss betrayed, no pain swiftly erased.
A wonder, how each leaden block of life
can be absorbed without a solid trace
into the human form. Ruin and grief
collapse inside us like great failing stars,
dark matter, dense and undetectable,
an inward spinning of the universe
that holds us at our core—still capable,
still moving on, skirting a dark that bends
and warps all light, on which all light depends.

Autumn in a Place without Winter

A subtle change has chipped the edge of things:
this quiet chill on pale blue cloud-streaked days;
the fog a harder shade of flinty gray.
A robin haunts the yard, but doesn't sing.
Dark berries fatten on their fronds again,
blood-red against the snow that never comes,
but somehow fills a presence in our bones:
white snows of memory. The first real rain
brings down a hail of leaves as green as spring
that bruise and darken on the asphalt drive.
You sweep the sodden deck, old shaker broom
worn jagged by the work. The season brings
no clarity, but this: we're here, alive,
aswirl in stir and stillness, light and gloom.

Fragment: Cycling Ascot Drive

Steepness gives us pretense to the air:
A winding roadway like a spiral stair
descends through treetops—eucalyptus, pine;
a hawk flies out beneath us, makes a line
and folds onto a limb, her black and white
a speckled camouflage in dappled light;
we're eye to eye, and then we sink below
and feel her eye upon us, take a slow
hard turn where rock and hillside drop away
to somewhere green and mystical. A gray,
chipped guardrail marks the edge where freedom takes
our breath, then sends it back: we ride the brakes,
hold closer to the pavement, circle down
to earth, and straightaway—and then, around
one curve, the brick and clamor of the town.

After a Rain, before Dark

After a rain, before dark, below a drape
of fog that fades the hills to shades of gray,
I walk out searching high—the tops of trees,
a patch of open sky, rooflines and wires,
the rust and green of redwood limbs in layers—
and scan for the eye that watches through the leaves
in camouflage, and almost turn away,
when black and brown resolve into the shape
of raptor, patterned wings appear, glide down,
incredibly, to light on grass and walk
among the ravens, feasting on the thick,
pale worms the flood has routed. Treading ground,
not humbled but aloof, red-shouldered hawk
now strides in robes of mist across the park.

Searching for the Slave Graveyard

Oak Ridge, Tennessee

Quickly we were lost. The woods fanned out
identically in all directions—these,
the winter woods of sycamore and oak,
of fallen bark and branches, and the wind
unsettling the accumulated leaves
that slowed our dragging feet: the shoosh of leaves

a thunder in our ears. We spiraled out,
and searched the woods for evidence—some wall,
or rotting fence, or any sign of work
or history—and pulled our sweaters tight
against a sharp November wind and pale
blue sky that filtered down through empty trees.

And here we stopped, and shuffled in those dry,
brown parchment leaves that gathered ankle deep,
and reveled in the noise; and then went on,
determined in some stubborn way. Our goal
dissolved among the trees. We circled on,
and marked a boulder streaked with quartz, and paused

to taste a wild persimmon's fallen fruit,
but found no path, no monument. These woods,
deciduous wild forest of our youth,
where we were pioneers, without a thought

to what had come before; where our small town
had sprung from nothing, servant to the war,

and so had time begun in our small lives,
where history had seemed a fantasy
of distant foreign worlds; our woods had held
a past we could not fathom, could not find.
Now chance had sent us here, these years too late,
an antique map: we spread it on the ground,

and traced a time before our lives, and names
long since erased, and towns and farms long gone
along the contours of our twenty miles
of Black Oak Ridge; and then familiar streets,
beginnings of our parents' legacy;
and then "slave graveyard," marked in broken lines.

We traced it with our fingertips. The wind
that moved the trees, that swirled the brittle leaves
around our feet, and swept through endless woods,
now queried what we sought, and offered up
a century of overgrowth and vines
and fallen logs. How quickly we were lost,

and questioning: it should have been just here,
just footsteps from the parking lot that showed
already on that nineteen-forties map,
a viewing ground that overlooked the dark
refinery that helped construct the bomb;
and questioning our purposes, our plan—

how simple, we had thought, to walk from line
to line through some unchanged ecology,
to move from darkened buildings to a time
so long ago surveyed and left to steep
in secrecy; how quickly it dissolved
and left us turning, questioning and lost;

how each successive growth supplants the last.
And soon we doubt our memories, the past,
the broken lines; doubt everything but wind
and fallen leaves, November chill and sky;
and find our way, return to easy lives,
and leave the woods to winter quietly.

Unforgiving

There is nothing more
than the fact of going on—
a moon in its orbit,
pulled and pulling;
a stone on its trajectory in space.
Each collision
is a pockmark,
a small but perceptible
change of path,
a lunar footprint
to last ten thousand years.
There can be no forgive
and forget.
We absorb what comes,
and hum with its vibrations—
one part per million is enough,
for that part has already
passed its wave
to the matrix.
What is remarkable
is how it is passed again
through generations:
mother to daughter,
daughter to child,
so that one day
decades hence,
a rushing well
of grief and rage
will open a sudden canyon
at your feet.

III

Waking on the Northwest Slope

There is no sunrise, this side of the hill—
only a sky on rheostat, whose light
increases to a slaty, waking white
with no known source, and leaves untouched the chill

laid down the night before. There is no ray
of warming sunlight bringing up a scene
of bench and garden, flagstone, fountain, green—
to lift me from my torpor into day.

But in the highest eucalyptus crown,
where fog has left its traces, gusty skies
stir up an icy show of scattered light:

a thousand golden suns reflected down
in pinpoint beams; and though I may not rise,
I know the East has seen the end of night.

Seasonal Song

What warm and spiny hope, what tiny glow
now kindles like a phosphorescent cell,
pale bioluminescence on a swell
of steely inner sea? Faint as a low
blue flame, it settles in, and left to grow
unchecked would spread its bloom across the tide,
bright streak of optimism just beside
the monstrous ocean's darkest ebb and flow.
Winter has struck the flint of this strange light,
has tricked the mind, and now the season's turn
means change is possible, and all that's fine
and clear may yet infuse a future bright
beyond all reason, "freeze" revised to "burn"
as easily as water, once, to wine.

December Meditation

The wood frog Rana sylvatica *embraces winter with its
ability to freeze solid without ill effect. Its organs are
infused with glucose, a natural antifreeze. Thawing on the
forest floor, it is often the first species to emerge in spring
for mating.*

How unfit we are for Zen:
warm-blooded,
bony-kneed,
at odds with winter.

One hard chill
and we roil with questions,
clamor with desires.

Even the willing monks
in Da Mo's time
were fitful and prone
to collapse,

and their heroes
to desperate acts:
razored eyelids,
severed limbs,
the snow made scarlet.

It is for Shen Kuang's arm
that the monks now greet
with one hand only.

Had he but turned that day
as he knelt in the cold,
laid eyes on a glistening frog,

understood its gift—
how it dons gelid winter
like a topcoat
of porcelain glaze—

surely the monks
would greet today
by pressing both their hands;

surely we'd meet the seasons' sway
with sweeter equanimity.

Crystalline

An ecologist found a blue pebble in the shape of a treefrog.
He carried it back to his lab—where it thawed and came
alive. It's now known that several species of frogs spend
their winters frozen.

Could I but give myself impassively
to ice and stillness, wintering upon
some pebble-scattered bank—what perfect peace.
The glaze of frost that coats this woodland stream

would settle, too, on me, encloak my dreams
in cold and stasis, quiet and surcease.
If I could be mistaken for a stone,
warm life made crystalline, how easily

dark weeks would pass, the frozen landscape drawn
so deep into my veins that we'd be one
and timeless. Then, the slightest hint of thaw

would animate again the power to draw
this glassy curtain from my eyes, to yawn
and breathe again as though you'd never gone.

Wakened by a Cricket at Dark, Jerusalem, 1975

Nothing cuts more cleanly through a dream
than pure sound: neither voice nor syllable,
but one clear note like glass made audible;
its strange, invasive presence fills the room,

takes hold the dream, bends closer to your ear;
you bolt awake—an upward rush of fear,
up to your feet, where, staggered, half aware,
you listen hard: pure silence. Cooling air

seeps in where night has gathered while you slept.
You puzzle over *what?* and, *who is there?*
This hazy patch of light—*window to where?*
Heart pounding still—*what enemy has slipped*

security and entered here? And then,
the sound again: it rises through the air,
a thrilling chain of vowels. The room comes clear,
and, now awake, you light a lamp, begin

the simple search: one rug, one chair, a desk;
pull out the bed, and there against the wall,
stock still and silent, near invisible,
the color of Jerusalem, of dust,

one tiny cricket. Somehow it has come
these thousand steps, three stories, down a hall,
matched to the rock fresh-hewn from ancient hills,
to trill the dark, and you, so far from home.

Dawn on a City of Dust

I have wanted to write
of Jerusalem.
But where my pen falls,
those great waves of history
would pull it under,
crush it under steel-link treads.

I have wanted to write
of such a small thing,
a brief moment
in a young life,
but when I raise my pen,
the city expands into the hills,
the hills into the past,
the past into ancient blood.

I have held for a quarter century
a certain dawn,
held it coiled in my hand,
cupped from the world's wind.
If I put it to words,
will the air degrade it
like an ancient manuscript
exposed?

I have walked in my mind
on that dawn path,
dust in my sandals
and a blue wind swirling

up from the thinning dark,
walked to the end
where the wall dropped off toward Judea,
and only the wind swept back,
and it was black.

But it was not black.
Such a simple thing:
the golden hour of dawn
on a city the color of dust,
haze of the coming heat,
the layers of houses,
pale and edged in shadows,
spilling down the hill
from the city wall.

I have wanted to tell
how the house lights flickered
like tiny golden flames,
how the first breath of day
extinguished them one by one;
how a slow donkey
and its master
set out to market.
But the flames rekindle,
and the city expands into fire,
and the fire into conflagration.

And to tell how the first sun
struck that great gold dome;
how a fig tree stood green

against the dust-colored stone;
how the fortress wall
rose like divine power
from the crumbling hills
in the pale dawn.

But as I raise my pen,
the sun on the dome
expands to a blinding white,
and the stones are shattered,
and a thousand hands
take the dust-colored shards
for weapons.

I have wanted to write
of such a small thing:
a shining moment
at dawn, mine alone,
shimmering beauty framed
in dust and light,
framed in my waking eyes.
But it is not mine.
And so the pen falls.

Lest I Forget You

In 1966, I soaked up joy
as the lawn soaked spray
from sprinklers turning rhythmically at night,
their hiss and pressure ticking me to sleep.
The world was sun, by day, and variegated flowers,
and orange groves between apartment houses
with thick-skinned sweets for taking;
and school a childish blur of sport and study,
and third-grade workbooks marked in ancient script,
the language a delightful puzzle;
and Fridays: *mischakei laila,* night games,
where even we, the youngest, could stay late
and rule the empty streets and darkened groves,
out in the night with crickets and croaking frogs.
Even on *shabbat,* jets thundered overhead.
All was exhilaration and strength.
And when we left, I took with me this idyll,
and dreamed I might return.

In 1974, I soaked grief from the air;
like a Red Sea sponge, had you squeezed me,
I would have wept salt to wounds,
not even knowing whose tears, whose heart.
Yet there was also joy: Jerusalem
of narrow streets, and markets piled with fruit,
embroidered cloth and honey-laden sweets,
that great, walled, ancient city with its power.

By day we studied history, and more than a few lies;
by night took nervous turns about the grounds
in pairs: one with an Uzi, one a horn
to guard against surprise.
And even we, the youngest, who had not
spent years at war, and not returned
with crooked bones and shoulders stitched with scars,
feigned age with thick sweet coffee, cigarettes,
and fidgety bravado. Jets swooped low
above the dorms in practice bombing runs,
then pulled up hard in dizzying arcs to the sky.
A year, and I returned home, thin as a survivor,
and laid myself on brick and ivy to dry.

In 1986, I soaked up rage,
though I did not want it,
and hardened my skin like coral shell against it.
Those places I had loved, the maze of streets
and ancient walls, the brightly colored markets,
now radiated tension like a heat.
Once, I had charmed my way in Arabic
past the patterned wares, into the shops,
to inner rooms and *kumkums* boiling water
for tea and cake and measured conversation.
Now words cleaved to my mouth; I could not speak.
And those who'd once been young with me
had aged, it seemed, a quarter century
for my twelve years. And jets ripped overhead,
their sound an anger mirrored in the stone

and bitter faces sipping bitter juices
against the battering sun. I let myself
be swept like a pebble down the dusty street
and out Damascus gate,
across the city and across the world
to home, where I could breathe.

In 1999, I soaked up news
as of a former lover,
whose passion one recalls in middle age
and cannot shake, despite old pain and conflict.
One questions those who've stuck it out together:
what must it be to live for generations
in such a place, with roots a thousand years
into an epic past, and for a future
now shattered like a wedding glass?
To live submerged, as Red Sea sponge or coral,
absorbing ocean tides of such extremes,
from highest joy to lowest grief and anger,
awash in tears, and nowhere for relief.
And then I saw my failing:
a living sponge does not soak up the sea,
but simply lives and breathes it,
as simply as I pulse with blood and air,
and can't transcend it. It falls to those like me
to lie down on the shores, watch jets pass over,
and serve the old, essential, sacred task
of sorrow and remembrance from afar.

Birds by the Bay

High tide, and the bay
like hammered metal shimmering,
light skimming away for miles,
depth surging landward in swells,
weighing against the shore,
pressing on those poor, slight
spindly-legged birds
whose high-pitched scurrying
peppered the sand at noon;
now they have flitted up
from the drowned beach
to perch on ill-fit stilts
in the lower limbs of cypress,
or huddle like stones among stones;
and above them, egrets
wispy as wind-blown scraps
caught up in green-dark branches.

An ocean looms within the bay,
rolls up from distant trenches
deep beyond the shelf;
great stacked boulders,
wet to the brink,
can barely hold it.
Cormorants stretch like arrows into flight,
aiming across continents;
gulls swirl in groups or wait in silence.

And on the air, a strange patrol
traces its glacial arcs, banks and slides
in smooth unison, dark platoon
of pelicans, jagged relics
whose huge span compasses the scene,
aloof, primeval,
more ancient than the people
who are gone from here.

Gradients

How do we find ourselves in this bright place?
—light fanning forward, darkness close behind,
damp scent of bay and oak. How did we find
the way to intersect here, face to face
upon a fault line, slipping at a pace
too subtle to detect?—and yet inclined
to follow it, urged onward by some blind
perception. Here, a slope, a slanting trace
of chimney smoke, crisscrossing with the sound
of distant traffic lanes; we, unaware
of gradients that wrap us in a weave
of push and pull—small force, and we are bound
like migratory birds to settle here,
as if we choose to stay, or choose to leave.

One's Own Kind

What company
does the goose find
in the flock?
What comfort
in this decagon
that glides across the lake
sans repartee,
a wordless unison
of self-sufficiencies.
I think of how, at
all odd hours,
I'd find you at the shop,
and silently
join in and set to work.

IV

Robins on Your Birthday

Why blue, the robin's egg?
—why bits of sky
instead of camouflage?

And why, from whence,
the dye for this
design extravagance?

And then, why earthworms,
rich as steak,
when other birds

will gladly make
their way on gnats or seeds?
And why more sung

than other breeds?
And why, today,
this madly cheerful song,

a whistled lunacy
outside my door
just after dawn

that first intrudes,
persists, and
breaking through,

now wakes me
from my torrid dreams
of you?

Desires Are Interchangeable

Desires are interchangeable. Take thirst:
a primal craving, surely; yet I pass
your door en route, and wanting in the worst
way just to quench my arid tongue, I cross
the threshold, and drink you, instead, for hours.
Take hunger: this sensation at my core
is plain and physical—and yet your powers
of interplay will fill me till no more
can enter, nor is wanted. And take greed:
my taste for fine possessions, which I keep
like treasures, has been traded for a need
of everything that's yours. And then, take sleep:
    I've found in waking all that rest requires—
    these dreams of you, these surfeited desires.

Love Sonnet

My love is like the Shostakovich Pre-
ludes Opus 34, his melody
a lilting line that spins and slips away
to reappear behind a minor key,
or tangled in the cord that lifts the blinds
upon a bright chromatic city view
(or dark and brooding night); whatever he finds
is made a dance: "Waltz of a Drunken Crew,"
"Three-Legged Polka"—joyous dissonance
in sudden tantrums of hilarity,
then liquid measures of sweet resonance
and tonic depth—a wild complexity
of twenty-four dimensions, half above
and half below G-flat. Such is my love.

A Homeopathy of the Spirit

By the Law of Similars, the jukebox dispenses
cheatin' songs for cheatin', heartbreak songs
for achings of the heart, jazz for the jitters and that
jagged counterpoint of deep, tormented soul;
hip-hop, of course, for rage, but if rage
and romance are both present: rock & roll—

this by the Rule of the Single Medicine, which also prescribes
oldies for heartbreak when it's steeped in nostalgia,
with or without regret. As for dose, as a matter
of principle, the amount must be infinitesimal,
arrived at through a series of dilutions so extreme
there may be no actual notes in the final medicinal solution—

from concentrated playings, quarter after quarter
in the downtown jukebox bar, decreasing repetitions
must be tapered down so far, till a resonance
is present even when the strains are gone; and now,
just reaching for the coin, you're pierced so keenly,
you cannot bear to put the music on.

The Spirit Changes

The spirit changes. Sometimes in the shock
of altered circumstance—just to survive.
The mind adjusts. The heart, wanting to live—
endure, that is—unrusts the frozen lock
you thought would never give. A gate swings through;
in place of grief, new possibility.
Like *that.* As though the heart and mind agree
to dial the world a few degrees askew
and call it normal. Sometimes, though, the dial
just slips—adaptive power becomes a kind
of glitch. You waken on the other shore,
the ocean to your left, your path a mile
off course—but you don't question what you find.
You think you just don't love him anymore.

No Love Lost

Love's never lost, but only stowed away
in darkened atria; it pulses there
unmarked, not quite forgotten. We're aware
of flutters now and then, but cannot say
just what the cause—a sound, a certain play
of light that pleases, or a smoky air
of possibility—a wisp is there
and gone, too thin to grasp. And then one day,
capriciously, it spills as if on cue
into an ordinary world of streets
and littered crosswalks, where a girl in blue
tight denim strides, black muscle shirt, slick part
and chiseled, boyish look, and almost meets
the old unguarded gaze of my changed heart.

Out Late in Summer

A glowing mist illuminates the street,
or so it seems, so magical the light
of street lamps on an August night. Not quite
thirteen, set loose, the freedom of bare feet
on pavement, buzzing insects, rare delight
of empty lanes, abandoned schoolyard, heat
and dark—forbidden smoke. Like cats, we meet,
assemble in the shadows, silent, slight
and furtive, keeping distance. But the thrill
of new connection flutters like the great
bright luna moth that flaps along the edge
of vision, brilliant, spinning in the thrall
of an imagined moon, quick like the heart
of someone poised for flight, perched on the verge.

Little Rock, July

Just one more sonnet on the summer heat,
the deafening cicadas and the *zzeerrr,*
zzeerrr, zzeerrr that weaves like metal through the air;
just one more poem is needed to the beat
of insect music, in the dreamy mist
that rises to the wires. Bright dragonflies
alight and flit and light again; gray skies
resolve to washed-out blue; the pulse persists
and amplifies toward evening in backyards
where neighbors idly linger, shape slow words
and cool their heads with lemonade, hard glass
pressed wet against the bone, bare feet in grass
alive with hoppers. Then the brilliant, clear,
high cardinal call cuts through it: *keer, keer, keer.*

The Goats Laboring

Trucked in like migrant workers, spindly legged
and eager, they assault the hill—once logged,
now thick with stumps and brush, and tinder-dry
brown grass: a day's assignment. Passersby
slow down in brief amusement at this sea
of motley goats let run amok, set free
to trample and devour. This is their task:
fight fire with hunger. Wearers of Satan's mask,
this cloven-hoofed and horned and bearded horde
consumes with fiery spirit all the hard
dry fuel that feeds the risk of conflagration
from one flicked ash. But what do they know of arson,
these ravenous goats? Hard at their urgent work,
which they pursue past daylight into dark,
they know but that they're hungry, and they eat.
Such is their nature—some would say the height
of wisdom. So accomplished at their job
are they, that any favored tree or shrub
worth sparing has been fenced, to keep in check
the all-outreaching, ever-craning neck
of goatly appetite. So stands the oak.

Next day, we find the hill transformed: now stripped
of brush and leaves, the grass completely cropped;
the laborers about in varied poses,
most lying, ruminating; some with noses
thrust deep in troughs of water or of feed

that supplements their diet of dry weeds;
some pose on stumps, hooves balanced on a point,
supporting keg-like bodies, every joint
a bony knob. One samples and rejects
a pungent eucalyptus shoot, inspects
and chews the bark that falls in leathery strips;
some, rampant, stretch to reach forbidden tips
of juniper and oak. A pair lock horns
like classic wrestlers on an ancient urn;
the young butt heads, with flat, thick skulls well-suited
to pointless conflict, pointedly disputed.
One elder turns on us a slit-eyed stare
of startling blue, his curly sheep-like hair,
an old man's coat. He seeks new leaves, so dense
and green just past the wires, but stops to sense
the tick, tick, tick of the electric fence.

A Red-Tailed Hawk Patrols

Easy circles, yes, but never *lazy*—
those lyrics have it wrong—each careless arc
an engine at its heart, a rust-red flame
of blood-red purpose. How deceptively
she glides along; then, almost sleepily,
a half-shrug, quarter-wingbeat fuels a climb
across the currents, past the ridgetop park
where treeline disappears into a hazy
gray September sky. She spirals back
with feathered legs suspended, searching eye
at work. How sweet the images we call on,
of parachutes and gliders: human stock;
we dream ourselves beneath her wings and fly,
forgetting beak, forgetting spur and talon.

Serena

The time of roses is gone. No more tending
that long bed beneath the telegraph wires,
the dark earth, the sharp thorns, the blooms ending

in late fall, time for pruning, the light bending
northward, and the first winter fires,
the time of roses gone. No more tending

side by side in spring, you and I, extending
fingertips to nip the buds, those quick desires
of dark earth, and sharp thorns, and blooms, ending

before they come to pass; we, the power, lending
extra strength to our few chosen flowers.
Now the time of roses is gone; no more tending

those perfect blossoms, cut early, you spending
their beauty in every room. And beauty requires
the dark earth, the sharp thorns, the blooms ending

too soon. Now gardeners bend, with silver light descending,
to turn the settled soil. The sun retires;
the time of roses is gone. No more tending
the dark earth, the sharp thorns, the blooms ending.

Retrospective

As quickly as a fragile spirit blinks
and fades into the blue fluorescent glow,
the hum of cold machines—as breathing sinks
and ceases under age's ravage—so

too, fade the bitter memories, the sole
persisting images nostalgic, sweet,
and sorely missed. Forgotten is the whole
dark warp of life. Instead, we weave deceit

and joy into a history our hearts
can bear—or, it is woven by those powers
that shield us from ourselves, obscure the parts
that threaten in survival's crucial hours:

the start, the finish—suffering replaced
like pangs of birth, the sting of death erased.

Signs and Symbols

Just home, suitcase still in hand, and we see
the tall eucalyptus has toppled down
our steep back slope, its great crown of leaves
filling what should have been the bright
sky above our patio, branches bowed taut against the glass
of the kitchen window and sliding door—

a miracle, really, that the door
didn't shatter—and we can see
now the oily, blue-green smears down the glass
from those pungent berries, and you put your suitcase down,
use the side door to step out into the bright
sunlit morning, face to face with a million misplaced leaves.

Just home from your father's funeral, and it leaves
us equally toppled and misplaced, up against a door
that has closed out of reach, as in a dream, its bright
light thinning to a slit before the click; and we can't help seeing
this huge tree as a kind of sign, coming down,
as it has, this dawn: great fallen life darkening the garden and the glass.

Here in the kitchen, I press my hand to the sliding glass
door where a flesh-colored limb flexes on the other side—like those leaves,
still full of doomed life—a limb the size of an arm reaching down
toward unaccustomed earth. I can almost feel a pulse through the door,
can barely, through the green filtered light, see
you outside, laying one hand on the trunk, shading your eyes from the brightness

with the other. There must have been a storm, and now this bright
sun cuts through the foliage, strikes the resilient glass,
and you, resilient as glass, out in the garden alone; I can see
your lithe figure moving, a shiver in the leaves
as you vault the fallen trunk, circle back toward the door,
studying how this tree came down,

how the highest limbs scraped down
the side of the house, leaving a bright
green trail that passes right over the doorbell
button. *It rang the bell!*—you laugh and tap on the glass
for me, and I leave
the green quiet of the kitchen to come see

the evidence—the sound of a downed tree falling: no crash, nor breaking glass,
but the bright sound of a doorbell in an empty house, leaving
the faintest echo, its mark on the door, a shimmer in the air that only you can see.

October, and the Owls

October, and the owls again—the chill
and smoke that filter through the terrace screen
are shadowed by a hint of sound. Between
faint calls, a hollow silence; and to will

the sound again, we lean onto the sill,
hold stiff and stop our breathing, strain to glean
some signal from the night. Outside, a scene
of moonlight, pine and cloud, and down the hill,

faint glimmer through the branches. Now, the far
dark bass vibration, syncopated, deep
as breath across some ancient vintner's glass,

king bottles played as flutes: old Melchior
and Jeroboam call across the steep
cool night in counterpoint—and fade—and pass.

Clair de Lune

I stop the car. Things can't be what they seem:
a spill of gold, as in a pirate's dream,
cascading down my driveway, glimmering
and flowing to the curb—my wedding ring,
too, catches in some light. And then I see:
high winds today have stripped the ginkgo tree
of all her brilliant yellow leaves at once—
a gust of sudden treasure to the ounce
of metal on my hand. And it occurs
to me, that phrase that commonly refers
to gold, "a yellow metal," never seemed
to capture it—for gold has weight, and sheen,
where yellow's just an easy streak of "bright"—
but now I learn, this strangely wind-lit night,
it's yellow mixed with moonshine that makes gold,
and spurs imagination to those old
heroic, dangerous quests of greed and sin.
I nod, switch off my headlights, and drive in.

Notes

p. 42: The epigraph is in the tone of the popular newspaper stories of the time. However, the primary source is Aparicio, S. et al., "Whole-genome shotgun assembly and analysis of the genome of Fugu rubripes," *Science,* vol. 297, no. 5585 (23 August 2002), pp. 1301–10.

p. 43: For a background on limb regeneration studies and supernumerary limbs, see Patrick W. Tank and Nigel Holder, "Pattern Regulation in the Regenerating Limbs of Urodele Amphibians," *The Quarterly Review of Biology,* Vol. 56, No. 2 (June 1981), pp. 113–142.

p. 57: Freeze tolerance in frogs has been widely known and studied since the publication of the paper W.D. Schmid, "Survival of frogs in low temperature," *Science,* vol. 215, no. 4533, (5 February 1982), pp. 697–698.

p. 59: The epigraph is based on informal accounts of the experience of Dr. William D. Schmid of the University of Minnesota, whose paper is cited above.

p.88: Very large wine bottles are sometimes named for biblical kings, with Jeroboam being a double magnum (3 liters) and Melchior, 18 liters.

A native of East Tennessee, D.R. Goodman now lives in Oakland, California, where she is founder and chief instructor at a martial arts school. Her poetry has appeared in such journals as *Crazyhorse, Notre Dame Review, Wisconsin Review, Cold Mountain Review, Whitefish Review,* and many others; and in the 2005 anthology, *Sonnets: 150 Contemporary Sonnets,* William Baer, editor. She is the author of *The Kids' Karate Workbook: A Take-Home Training Guide for Young*  *Martial Artists,* from North Atlantic/Blue Snake Books; and of an illustrated chapbook, *Birds by the Bay.*

    Greed: A Confession was a finalist for the 2013 Able Muse Book Award.

Photo by Linda Nikaya

CPSIA information can be obtained at www.ICGtesting.com
Printed in the USA
BVOW03s1529210914

367462BV00004B/18/P